YOUR KNOWLEDGE HAS VALUE

- We will publish your bachelor's and master's thesis, essays and papers

- Your own eBook and book - sold worldwide in all relevant shops

- Earn money with each sale

Upload your text at www.GRIN.com
and publish for free

Formation of Catholic Priests as Artisanal and not Policing

Pope Francis and the Formation of Catholic Priests for the 21st Century

Tarcisius Mukuka

Bibliographic information published by the German National Library:

The German National Library lists this publication in the National Bibliography; detailed bibliographic data are available on the Internet at http://dnb.dnb.de.

ISBN: 9783346312914
This book is also available as an ebook.

© GRIN Publishing GmbH
Nymphenburger Straße 86
80636 München

All rights reserved

Print and binding: Books on Demand GmbH, Norderstedt, Germany
Printed on acid-free paper from responsible sources.

The present work has been carefully prepared. Nevertheless, authors and publishers do not incur liability for the correctness of information, notes, links and advice as well as any printing errors.

GRIN web shop: https://www.grin.com/document/962848

Formation of Catholic Priests as Artisanal and not Policing
Pope Francis and the Formation of Catholic Priests for the 21st Century

By Dr Tarcisius Mukuka

> If the seminary is too large, it must be divided into communities with formators capable of truly accompanying people. Dialogue must be serious, fearless, and sincere. And we must consider that the language of young people in formation today is different from that of those who preceded them: we are living in a changed epoch. Formation is an artisanal job, non-policing [*Se il seminario è troppo grande, bisogna dividerlo in comunità con formatori capaci di seguire davvero le persone. Il dialogo deve essere serio, senza paura, sincero. E bisogna considerare che il linguaggio dei giovani in formazione oggi è diverso da quello di chi li ha preceduti: viviamo un cambiamento d'epoca. La formazione è un'opera artigianale, non poliziesca*].[1]

1. Introduction

The title of this article is a double-edged sword. As formation is artisanal, it is open to creativity by both providers and beneficiaries. The sky is literally the limit of what it can achieve, especially when those who accompany seminarians or any other candidates in formation, are mature and integrated formators. That is the upside. The *Oxford Dictionary* defines artisanal as "relating to or characteristic of an artisan, of a product, especially food or drink, made in a traditional or non-mechanised way." That is the way I liked my daily ice-cream in Rome. That is how I like my priests to be made — home-made. The formator is an artisan who is skilled in the art of human-spiritual whispering. He is like the traditional healer we call *shing'anga*[2] in Zambia. You know he or she is good even though they have not been to medical school. The human-spiritual whisperer is good even though he has not been to graduate school. That is the upside and main point of this article. The downside is that sometimes providers can get it horribly wrong when formators are factory mass manufacturers as we did in May 1985 when an entire cohort of 67 seminarians went on strike and were subsequently all fired in a draconian display of hard power (Mukuka 2020 forthcoming)[3] in an ecclesiastical version of product recall. As in 1985, when the formators are the wrong fit, this is a recipe for disaster. You have to admit that some so-called formators are not up to the task. Some of them are in the seminary as the equivalent of being sent to the naughty corner or to Siberia. Word does get around. A priest is sent to the seminary because either he can't stand his bishop or vice versa or he is unsuitable for the parish so that ironically, he can go and prepare those to take over from him. I for one did not think I was mature enough to accompany others. The idea of spending 24 hours letting students walk in my moccasins and I, in theirs, was not particularly attractive to me. I preferred an arrangement where non-academic formators, especially prepared for the task, to do the job and academic lecturers parachuted in from the outside for the purpose while also teaching at other tertiary institutions so as to support themselves.

This article takes a leaf from Pope Francis' concern about initial formation for the priesthood, evidenced at the head of this article and suggests in the light of the *Ratio Fundamentalis* (2016) that formators avoid mass manufacture but focus on "small is beautiful" accompaniment and discernment, seeing formation as *un'opera artigianale* [an artisanal job]. The adjective *artigianale* was one of the earliest I learnt when I arrived in Rome. I first came across it for the first at an Ice-cream bar on *Via delle Fornaci*, 00165 Roma. I asked the young lady behind the counter what made it special, she told me "*È gelato artigianale* [It is home-made ice-cream]. The priest of the 21st century ought to be *artigianale* [home-made] and not factory-made. Failure to do this, risks, in the words of the Pontiff, breeding *piccoli mostri* [little monsters] in circumstances that are akin to policing [*poliziesca*] or correctional services rather than emancipative and transformative Gospel-led formation. As the Pope says, formation "is a work of art, not policing" [*è un'opera artigianale, non poliziesca*],[4] echoed by Sister Maryasia Weber (2018). This article is something of a mixed bag. Although broken, the system of formation still manages to produce masterpieces every now and again but one feels that like a student's end of term evaluation, "the system could do better."

This article is about formation as an art, towards evangelical empowerment driven by the Nazareth *Manifesto* through accompaniment and discernment by mature mentors who are human-spiritual whisperers of their charges. I was beginning to get paranoid at the number of times the word "rotten" or "broken" pops into my head in reference to the priestly formation system until my friend Elizabeth Mphande told me in an email, "It's really sad and pathetic. It's like the whole system is rotten and some guys are just out there to do a job to get easy money from parishioners. Some of these guys are practically full-time married men who just come and say Mass from time to time" (email, 1 July 2020). Marie Ngandwe, not her real name, echoed a similar frustration when she wrote to me.

> It's very unfortunate that some of our priests who have children abandon them in preference to their priestly vocation. Some of our priests have made women pregnant and told them to abort and some die along the way. It's so sad that this has caused many deaths while some are still serving as priests. I witnessed one occasion where a priest told his girlfriend to abort for fear the child would resemble him. This poor woman was even infected with *HIV/AIDS* and later on died. Our priests are sexually active but they hide themselves behind their Roman collars. God knows that I'm not judging them but that is the truth. Most religious sisters become pregnant, they abort and the priests are the instigators (email, 1 January 2020).

Presumably, the priests in question went through a priestly formation that prides itself in forming them to preach an "*evangelium vitae*" [Gospel of life], both in word and deed, in which abortion is not only sinful but attracts automatic excommunication [*latae sententiae*]. As Catholic priests trained in the era of John Paul II, they also studied the theology of the body and sexual ethics in which life begins at the moment of conception. No priesthood is worth its name in whatever currency, if it is achieved and maintained at the expense of aborted foetuses. It is, as the King James Bible puts it, "thy brother's [or sister's] blood crieth unto me from the ground" (Gen 4.10 *KJV*). I couldn't care less how divided scientists and ethicists are on when life begins, whether it is at implantation of the fertilised ovum in the uterus or even when ensoulment takes place. Human life cannot be reduced to an equation or scientific hypothesis. The Catholic priest ought to be in the forefront of a Gospel of life from womb to tomb. When in doubt, it is better to err on the side of an abundance of caution.

2. Formators as Human-Spiritual Whisperers

Before I develop the concept of the formator as a human-spiritual whisperer, I want to begin with what a formator should not be. This profile must be taken alongside one that I develop below in the section "Little Monsters Look Like This." The formator must not be a careerist and clericalist. The same goes for his bishop who appoints him to his ministry. Addressing bishops at St Peter's Square on 5 November 2014 during a Wednesday General Audience, Pope Francis did not mince his words, words particularly pertinent to formators as human-spiritual whisperers concerning clericalism. He categorised clericalism as a negative pathway to sterile authoritarian and ecclesiastical careerism, privilege, entitlement and power and hard power for that matter, if I may add, as I have argued elsewhere (Mukuka 2020).[5] "It's sad when you see a man who seeks this office and who does so much to get there and when he makes it, he doesn't serve, but struts like a peacock, living only for his own vanity,"[6] the Pope said in his usual colourful language.

Most of what I am hoping to say about priestly formation and the type of Church needed to get there I found very well summarised in an abstract for a *Teologiese Studies/Theological Studies* article, "The Catholic Church in need of de-clericalisation and moral doctrinal agency: Towards an ethically accountable hierarchical leadership" by Jennifer Slater which I am going to cite here at length. My reason for citing it is to agree with it that clericalism is the *bête noire* of the Catholic Church.

> Under normal circumstances the Church would function as an agent of change and transformation, but this article focuses on the Church herself that needs radical change if she is to remain relevant in mission and ministry in this current era. Clericalism and the centralisation of hierarchical control can be identified as the root causes of institutional pathology and weakening collegiality. To address clericalism may require the adjustment of seminary training, as in the current system seminarians are nurtured in a sense of separateness, promoting male ego and feed gender exclusivity and doctrinal self-righteousness. While the seminary was once an instrument of reform in the Catholic Church, established to counter problems such as clerical concubinage and illiteracy, but now it is no longer suitable as it has become the forum that breeds other problems. Priority attention should be paid to purge the Church of rampant

> clericalism, discriminatory scapegoating of gay persons, marginalisation of free thinkers, exclusion of women priests, the perceived moral laxity of family life issues and reception of communion by divorced Catholics without the benefits of annulment. Discrediting the personal authority of the pope is hardly an enlightened option. What ought to be transformed is the centralisation of control and allowing increased localised dominion whereby crises such as sexual abuse scandals could be addressed and solved more speedily and liberally, and limit the need to go to the top for solutions. To wait for centralised, hierarchal structures to deal with urgent issues is not desirable, as speedy accountability is needed to address issues that hurt the Church in its entirety.[7]

I could not have put it better myself but soon after the abstract, Jennifer Slater commits a couple of errors of fact and attribution in her article. She quotes Carol Glatz, *Catholic News Service* Rome correspondent as, "in his speech, 'Bishops must be servants, not vain careerists after power, honour.'" Carol Glatz is actually a she and the speech title is the title of her article for the *National Catholic Reporter*. Jennifer Slater then proceeds to quote Carol Glatz but what she gives is a short medley from Pope Francis' speech to the bishops at a Wednesday General audience of 5 November 2014. So, rather than repeat her quotation medley, I am going to quote directly from the Pope's address in Italian followed by my translation. I give this lengthy quotation to underscore Pope Francis' opposition to careerism and clericalism in the Catholic Church — the two cardinal sins, the two *bêtes noires*, to be avoided by the formator as a human-spiritual whisperer.

> *Comprendiamo, quindi, che non si tratta di una posizione di prestigio, di una carica onorifica. L'episcopato non è un'onorificenza, è un servizio. Gesù l'ha voluto così. Non dev'esserci posto nella Chiesa per la mentalità mondana. La mentalità mondana dice: "Quest'uomo ha fatto la carriera ecclesiastica, è diventato vescovo". No, no, nella Chiesa non deve esserci posto per questa mentalità. L'episcopato è un servizio, non un'onorificenza per vantarsi. Essere Vescovi vuol dire tenere sempre davanti agli occhi l'esempio di Gesù che, come Buon Pastore, è venuto non per essere servito, ma per servire (cfr Mt 20,28; Mc 10,45) e per dare la sua vita per le sue pecore (cfr Gv 10,11). I santi Vescovi – e sono tanti nella storia della Chiesa, tanti vescovi santi – ci mostrano che questo ministero non si cerca, non si chiede, non si compra, ma si accoglie in obbedienza, non per elevarsi, ma per abbassarsi, come Gesù che «umiliò se stesso, facendosi obbediente fino alla morte e a una morte di croce» (Fil 2,8). E' triste quando si vede un uomo che cerca questo ufficio e che fa tante cose per arrivare là e quando arriva là non serve, si pavoneggia, vive soltanto per la sua vanità* [We must understand therefore, that this [the episcopacy] is not a prestigious position, an honorific position. The episcopate is not an honour, it is a service. Jesus wanted it so. There must be no place in

the Church for the worldly mentality. The worldly mentality says: "This man has achieved this ecclesiastical career; he has become bishop." No, no, there must be no place in the Church for this mentality. The episcopate is a service, not an honour for bragging rights. Being Bishops means always keeping in front of your eyes the example of Jesus who, as Good Shepherd, came not to be served, but to serve (cf Mt 20,28; Mk 10,45) and to give his life for his sheep (cf. Jn 10,11). The holy bishops — and there are many in the history of the Church, many holy bishops — show us that this ministry is not sought, asked, or bought, but welcomed in obedience, not to elevate oneself, but to lower oneself, like Jesus who "humbled himself, making himself obedient until death and death on the cross" (Phil 2,8). It is sad when you see a man looking for this office and doing many things to get there and when he gets there, he doesn't serve but struts his stuff like a peacock, living only for his own vanity].[8]

Perhaps it is worth our while to cite the text of Titus 1.5–9, which Pope Francis used in his 5 November 2014 Wednesday General audience address to the bishops. If it was up to me to look for qualities of human-spiritual whisperers, and indeed of bishops in general, that is where I would direct anyone interested.

> [5] The reason I left you in Crete was that you might put in order what was left unfinished and appoint elders [πρεσβυτέρους] in every town, as I directed you. [6] An elder must be blameless, faithful to his wife, a man whose children believe and are not open to the charge of being wild and disobedient. [7] Since an overseer [ἐπίσκοπον] manages God's household, he must be blameless — not overbearing, not quick-tempered, not given to drunkenness, not violent, not pursuing dishonest gain. [8] Rather, he must be hospitable, one who loves what is good, who is self-controlled, upright, holy and disciplined. [9] He must hold firmly to the trustworthy message as it has been taught, so that he can encourage [παρακαλεῖν] others by sound doctrine and refute those who oppose it (Titus 1.5–9 *NIV*).

This was either ironic or tongue in cheek of the Pope to choose to address celibate bishops by choosing a text that enjoins them to be faithful to their wives, "An elder must be blameless, faithful to his wife, a man whose children believe and are not open to the charge of being wild and disobedient" (Titus 1.6). Purely on that score, none of the episcopal and sacerdotal cassocks surrounding him qualified. Perhaps this was an unintended telegraph about the *viri probati* we have heard so much about but ultimately Pope Francis failed to deliver in *Querida Amazonia*. But I am grateful to Jennifer Slater for her article and I now want to underscore the principal areas of agreement with her and their relevance to the formator as human-spiritual whisperer.

The seminary human-spiritual whisperer must not be a clericalist. The problem with the clericalist is that he is not in it for the sake of the Gospel. St Paul's advice cited by Pope Francis to the bishops above must be his or her guide but is not. "He must hold firmly to the trustworthy message as it has been taught, so that he can encourage [παρακαλεῖν] others by sound doctrine and refute those who oppose it" (Titus 1.9 *NIV*). He does not sound like the 26-year-old newly ordained *arrogante* I was when I was appointed for the task. If he or she is a clericalist, they will model and encourage "separateness, promoting male-ego and feed gender exclusivity and doctrinal self-righteousness" (Slater 2019), especially in all-male formation team. I am particularly eager to underscore, unlike the Vatican deep state, that Pope Francis is not part of the problem but part of the solution to formation as human-spiritual whispering. Clearly, as we shall see shortly, George Weigel begs to differ. But as Jennifer Slater points out, "Discrediting the personal authority of the Pope is hardly an enlightened option. What ought to be transformed is the centralisation of control and allowing increased localised dominion whereby crises such as sexual abuse scandals could be addressed and solved more speedily and liberally, and limit the need to go to the top for solutions" (Slater 2019) as did both John Paul II and Benedict XVI. George Weigel is by all accounts a John Paul II Papist. He is the author of *Witness to Hope: The Biography of Pope John Paul II* (1999). It is a pity Jennifer Slater uses a word that is antithetical to the spirit of servant leadership, "dominion."

During the pontificates of John Paul II (1978–2005) and Benedict XVI (2005–2013), the Catholic Church suffered from precisely that spirit of dominion in which centralisation and hard power were used in an anal-retentive manner. Solving the many problems that plague the Catholic Church requires first, "de-patriarchalisation" of the Church and devolution of power from the apex of the pyramid to the base or alternatively just inverting the whole pyramid. This would require formators who are human-spiritual whisperers of this inverted pyramid, formators who are schooled in the use of Gospel-like soft power and servant leadership. On de-patriarchalisation of the Church as a way to human-spiritual whispering in the Church, even without reading George Weigel's *The Next Pope* (2020), my view is that this book is unlikely to contribute to human-spiritual whispering. I am basing my prejudice on John J. Strynkowski's review of the book which I find persuasive.[9] And here is why I am not recommending *The Next Pope*.

> In his new book *The Next Pope*, George Weigel seeks to create a profile of the next pope. The profile he establishes can be easily summarised: "not Pope Francis." The book is a hardly subtle critique of the present bishop of Rome. In a brief 133 pages I counted at least 62 times when he used the verb "must" in regard to what the next pope should do (*Ibid*).

A quick perusal of the table of contents convinces me that George Weigel's next Pope is preferably a John Paul II or his clone, Benedict XVI. Both Popes were associated with the new Evangelisation and an authoritarian, patriarchal view of the Church which was part of the problem in the first place. Arguably, the birthplace of the new evangelisation is not even Rome but *Nowa Huta* near Krakow, where Karol Wojtyla grew up. During his first apostolic pilgrimage to Poland, during

Holy Mass at the shrine of the Holy Cross on 9 June 1979, John Paul II announced the birth of the new evangelisation.

> The new wooden Cross was raised not far from here at the very time we were celebrating the Millennium. With it we were given *a sign* that on the threshold of the new millennium, in these new times, these new conditions of life, the Gospel is again being proclaimed. *A new evangelization* has begun, as if it were a new proclamation, even if in reality it is the same as ever. The Cross stands high over the revolving world (John Paul II 1979: par 1 — italics in the original).

The term "new evangelisation" was subsequently made popular by Pope John Paul II who used it during an address to the Latin American bishops in Port-au-Prince, Haiti on 9 May 9 1983. He declared that the fifth centenary of the first evangelisation of the Americas (1492–1992) should mark the beginning of a new era of evangelization. Pope John Paul II then expounded on the idea later, in his encyclical, *Redemptoris Missio*, which became the *Magna Carta* of the new evangelisation. He did the same in his apostolic letter, *Tertio Millennio Adveniente*, issued for the Great Jubilee of the year 2000 and his apostolic exhortation, *Novo Millennio Ineunte*. In 2010, Pope John Paul II's protégé, Benedict XVI established the *Pontifical Council for Promoting the New Evangelization*. When he called for the Year of Faith (2012–2013) on the 50th anniversary of the Second Vatican Council, he opened it with a general assembly of the Synod of Bishops on the new evangelization for the transmission of the Christian faith.[10]

The purpose of the above short excursus is to give context to George Weigel's the *Next Pope* but I remain personally unpersuaded that a John Paul II or Benedict XVI *redivivus* as the next Pope is the tonic the Church of the future needs. Their Church was too rear-guard for the ecclesial and societal challenges of the twenty-first century. I agree with Michael Sean Winters who opines that "George Weigel's latest book, *The Next Pope: The Office of Peter and a Church in Mission*, is a thin one at only 141 pages. But it is thin, too, in the sense that what it communicates is either a repeat of Weigel's earlier themes or a recantation of ideas — some of which are true but banal and others are misleading and given to caricature. The only real novelty is the degree to which he casts aspersions on the current Pope with catty insinuations without sufficient courage to say plainly where he thinks Pope Francis has erred."[11] Michael Sean Winters rightly criticises "the chapter on the fullness of the Catholic faith" in which George Weigel "pens a series of assertions about what the new Pope needs to do that are really passive-aggressive attacks on Francis" and the blather about "the heroic priesthood" which "is part and parcel of the clerical culture that must be uprooted, not indulged."[12] I wish George Weigel would balance this with some serious *apologia* for the "heroic laity" who are often the heroes of the faith and I have seen a good few in my lifetime. I think his "heroic priesthood" is often synonymous with a "pampered priesthood." A lay-centred Church is the way forward and what the next Pope should be about.

In view of the above, Cardinal Timothy Michael Dolan of New York, who at 70, could be casting his ballot at the next conclave has committed a *faux pas* by sending copies of the *Next Pope* to all the cardinals.[13] Bang out of order if you ask me. What was he thinking? I am now putting him on my list of the Vatican deep state who are hell-bent on thwarting Bergoglian reforms. In case you think I am unfair to George Weigel, here he is in his own words on why he wrote the *Next Pope* followed by a justification of his long-time pal and theological stablemate, Timothy Dolan endorsing the book as it was sent to the cardinals.

> Some Catholics, often found in the moribund local Churches of western Europe, claim that the Council's "spirit" has never been implemented (although the Catholic Lite implementation they propose seems more akin to liberal Protestantism than Catholicism). Other voices claim that the Council was a terrible mistake and that its teaching should be quietly forgotten, consigned to the dustbin of history. In the *Next Pope: The Office of Peter and a Church in Mission* (just published by Ignatius Press), I suggest that some clarifying papal interventions are needed to address these confusions.

> Thus, the next pope ought to insist that the Catholic Church does not do rupture, reinvention, or "paradigm shifts." Why? Because Jesus Christ — "the same yesterday and today and forever" (Hebrews 13.8) — is always the centre of the Church. That conviction is the beginning of any authentic evangelization, any authentically Catholic development of doctrine, and any proper implementation of Vatican II.[14]

> It's ridiculous. I don't recall anyone making such a silly criticism when Peter Hebblethwaite and Luigi Accattoli wrote books about the future of the papacy during the pontificate of John Paul II.[15]

> A 'speechless' cardinal may be something of an ontological impossibility, and in any event these 'speechless' cardinals seemed to find their voices when they wanted to. As I indicated previously, Cardinal Dolan didn't send them my book; Ignatius Press sent them my book and the cardinal kindly provided a cover letter thanking Ignatius Press for making the book available to the College of Cardinals. So, if anyone was struck 'speechless' by Cardinal Dolan 'sending' them a book, they ought to look again at his letter and read it accurately this time.[16]

Cardinal Timothy Dolan's "letter" was a one-liner, "I am grateful to Ignatius Press for making this important reflection on the future of the Church available to the College of Cardinals."[17] I think "Catholic Lite" is George Weigel's pot-shot at Francis. My only problem with his passive-aggressive anti-Francis narrative is the underlying assumption that the issue is whether Vatican II has been implemented or not and the best hope for implementing Vatican II is a John Paul II or a Benedict XVI *redivivus* as mentioned above. I am just surprised that 55 years after the end of Vatican II, George Weigel should still be harping on about Vatican II. Whether Vatican II has been implemented or not, I think it is time we started talking about Vatican III and from where I am sitting, Pope Francis is our best bet for pulling that cat out of the bag. But I have a feeling we may be waiting until the cows come home, to conflate feline and bovine metaphors. In the meantime, clericalism continues to rule the roost.

Many seminarians come looking for the trappings of George Weigel's "heroic priesthood" as an elite and clerical career that is better than the life they have left behind in their rural hinterlands. As Swithan Kalobwe put it in his powerful testimony, "In rural Zambia, Catholic missionaries, who were ordinarily white fathers both in race and missionary order, lived a life notably better than the majority of the local population. That in itself, though unintended, was inspiring to many young Catholics, like myself, to admire the priesthood. I cannot tell whether I was a victim of that, but in any case, I got a lot of interest in the priesthood and subsequently started taking steps into priestly formation."[18] I can tell. Most of us begin with admiring the trappings that include the cassock, the car, to be fair also sometimes the holiness of life but this admiration is a mixed bag. For some, it is the socio-economic package that predominates and for others it is the obsequiousness with which the priest is worshipped. The irony for the white missionary is that the life we admired of him was by comparison to where he was coming from nothing short of pre-industrial and rustic. A good human-spiritual whisperer will help to refine that initial glass-eyed view of the priest, principally through the example of his own simple life. Ironically, as a formator, although I did not evince affluence, a T shirt I used to wear promoting a better life for the subaltern of the Copperbelt, became a fashion statement for the priesthood as a better life to aspire to, however that better life was understood.

3. The Metaphor of a Formator as a Human-Spiritual Whisperer

The metaphor of a formator as a human-spiritual whisperer may not make immediate sense if the reader is not familiar with the horse whisperer metaphor. The *horse whisperer* is a famous 1998 American drama film directed by and starring Robert Redford, one of my favourite American actors. I first saw him on the big screen in *Out of Africa* — a 1985 American epic romantic drama film directed and produced by Sydney Pollack, and starring Robert Redford[19] and Meryl Streep — my first onscreen girlfriend I first met in Kramer vs. Kramer, a 1979 American legal drama film written and directed by Robert Benton, based on Avery Corman's 1977 novel of the same name starring Dustin Hoffman and Meryl Streep. *Out of Africa* is based loosely on the 1937 autobiographical book *Out of Africa* written by Isak Dinesen, the pseudonym of Danish author Karen Blixen, with additional material from Isak Dinesen's 1960 book *Shadows on the Grass* and other sources. But back to the *horse whisperer*, the book was based on the 1995 novel the *Horse Whisperer* by Nicholas Evans. In the movie, Robert Redford plays the title role of the *Horse Whisperer* in which he is presented as a talented trainer with a remarkable gift for understanding horses. This is the clue to our metaphorical analogy of the formator as a human -spiritual whisperer. His or her job is to train but this profession is almost an inborn charism for connecting and understanding other human beings. In the movie the *Horse Whisperer*, Robert Redford is hired to help an injured teenager, played by one of my big screen girlfriends, Scarlett Johansson and her horse back to health following a tragic accident. The candidate who comes to the seminary is a bit like an injured horse being nursed back to full health. The formator accompanying the candidate needs special skills. Every candidate carries a baggage of hurt and dysfunction that need healing before the candidate is able to perform optimally. I made this point to an ex-seminarian who was contemplating returning to the seminary after the bishop had declared doubts about his suitability and he was not amused. Two things worried me: he had not done anything with his life in four years and listening to him convinced me he had issues including alcoholism which needed addressing. I was afraid he may be seeing the priesthood as an easier option. The formator needs to be a talented trainer with a remarkable gift for understanding human beings and sniffing out problem cases such as my friend. I fear no such atmosphere exists. Instead candidates are encouraged to pretend while investing in a proverbial chastity belt which is jettisoned the same day they are ordained and live out their days "from bed linen to Altar linen," usually not alone in the case of the former.

If the truth be told, although I like to describe my 7-year career in the seminary as a formator, I was more an academic lecturer and if the testimonies of my former students are to be believed, I was not half as bad. But formation was a head-trip for me. I loved living in my head and enthusing others to do the same more than being a human-spiritual whisperer. Being a true formator or a human-spiritual whisperer is a different ball game. It requires first and foremost, patience to start scratching the surface and get to the real gem. Many seminarians, due to fear, do not allow themselves to be refined. For that you need the fire and ironically for *Mpima*, that was the motto, *ignem mittere in terram* [to cast fire upon the earth]. Not just upon the earth, but deep into the recesses of the would-be priest. According to the *Oxford Dictionary*, a whisperer is "a person skilled in taming or training a specified kind of animal, typically using body language and gentle vocal encouragement rather than physical contact" like Robert Redford in the *Horse Whisperer*. The formator is a human-spiritual whisperer and I am not so sure I was able to rise to such dizzy heights. Of the dozen or so fellow-formators I worked with over the 7-year period, I can mention only one who struck me as a potential or actual human-spiritual whisperer, a gentle American by the name of John Jack O'Leary from Spokane, Washington, a man ironically with the experience of actual horses when he was growing up. He was as down to earth as the rural earth of Mpima ward where our seminary was situated. And sometimes he would walk bare foot, literally, to be down to earth. I borrow the idea of a human-spiritual whisperer from another American, Steven Keyl who explains the concept as follows.

> Dog and horse whisperers alike are experts. For the rest of us, the animals we spend the most time with are other people. So, to maximize our effectiveness with others it makes sense to cultivate the same skills as the animal whisperers — to become in the truest sense, a "Human Whisperer."[20]

4. Do not call anyone on earth 'father'

On the role of the formator as human-spiritual whisperer and the *bête noire* of clericalism, discussion is still incomplete if it does not factor in the small matter of titles such as "His Excellency," or "My Lord" or even "Father." This issue is bound to split priests in half but hear me out all the same. If jettisoning such clericalist titles will go a long way in proclaiming Galatian egalitarianism, then perhaps it will not be in vain. Let me put my cards on the table on this matter. Even as an active Catholic priest, soon after my ordination, I started waging an ultimately unsuccessful personal crusade against my ecclesiastical family so that it might jettison the patriarchal, godfather-like title "Father" for the priest and the address "My Lord" for the bishop and replace them with "brother" as in the Franciscan sense of Friar. The titles "His Excellency," or "My Lord" or even "Father" belong to a pernicious, patriarchal, paternalistic and bygone feudal era that is best left bygone. I think Jesus was rightly concerned that such titles might go to the head of some recipients who may be tempted to take the place of God. I know, titles do not a priest make but they say a lot about what pedestal we would like to sit on. This is often the case of well-meaning Catholic priest who begin to refer to themselves in the third person.

In the light of the subject I moot above, I hesitate to wheel in Mt. 23.9 which forbids us to call anyone on earth our "father" but for a change I am inclined to agree with my Protestant friends here, such as the ministry that goes by the name *Verse by Verse Ministry International* which describes itself as "a non-profit, non-denominational, unaffiliated Christian ministry that is dedicated to promoting the preaching and teaching of God's Word clearly and boldly."[21] I was called "father" for 14 years but I can't say hand on heart that I found the title helpful apart from perpetuating patriarchy — but to give the discussion context, I will quote a bigger chunk than is the usual Protestant proof text practice.

> **23** Then Jesus said to the crowds and to his disciples: **²** "The teachers of the law and the Pharisees sit in Moses' seat. **³** So you must be careful to do everything they tell you. But do not do what they do, for they do not practice what they preach. **⁴** They tie up heavy, cumbersome loads and put them on other people's shoulders, but they themselves are not willing to lift a finger to move them.
>
> **⁵** "Everything they do is done for people to see: They make their phylacteries wide and the tassels on their garments long; **⁶** they love the place of honour at banquets and the most important seats in the synagogues; **⁷** they love to be greeted with respect in the marketplaces and to be called 'Rabbi' by others.
>
> **⁸** "But you are not to be called 'Rabbi,' [Ραββί] for you have one Teacher [διδάσκαλος], and you are all brothers [ἀδελφοί]. **⁹** And do not call anyone on earth 'father' [πατήρ], for you have one Father [πατήρ], and he is in heaven. **¹⁰** Nor are you to be called instructors [καθηγηταί], for you have one Instructor [καθηγητὴς], the Messiah. **¹¹** The greatest among you will be your

servant. [12] For those who exalt themselves will be humbled, and those who humble themselves will be exalted (Mt 23.1–11 *NRSV*).

Being an exegete as my day job, my hermeneutics of suspicion tells me that Jesus is more than just stating the literal truth here. In fact, he is not being literal. Presumably, he did not have qualms about referring to Mary and Joseph as "mother and father." He wants to get to the significance of titles or their propensity to be abused. It is that significance that Jesus is trying to warn against than the titles *per se*. This is my nuanced answer to the question, "Should we take literally Jesus' command to 'not call anyone on earth your father'?" My answer is that probably in a worldly and even biological senses of the word "father," you are at liberty to call anyone "father" and in fact, should. I don't think my son would agree to call me anything other than dad. We are in the process of deciding what my granddaughter should call me. I am toying with a shortened version of grandpa such as "Paps." But in the spiritual sense of "father" as in "Our Father who art in heaven," only God deserves to be called "father." It is in this sense, and only in this sense, you may not call anyone "father." How that works out in practice, I have no idea but from where I am sitting, it is just as easy not to ascribe the title "father" except your biological or adopted "father" and only in the worldly sense. The spiritual sense should only be reserved to God. This is how my Protestant friends from *Verse by Verse Ministry International* explain this and for a change I concur.

> Since each of these titles already belongs to a member of the Godhead, we ought not take them for ourselves nor confer them upon another in a spiritual context. Therefore, the proper interpretation of this passage understands that these terms are prohibited in a religious context. For example, Christians may not address a Catholic priest as "father" nor a Protestant pastor as a spiritual "leader" nor even a Sunday school instructor as our spiritual teacher. Instead, we acknowledge the Godhead alone in these things.[22]

Suppose you agree with me and my *Verse by Verse Ministry International* brothers, you might be interested in my proposal for an alternative to "father" in the Catholic Church. I have a perfectly good alternative in a biblical title, "brother" [ἀδελφός] or even "sister" [ἀδελφή] when the time comes to ordain women. The day after I was ordained a priest, my bishop had one advise for me. "Treat younger men as brothers [ἀδελφούς], older women as mothers [μητέρας], and younger women as sisters [ἀδελφὰς], with absolute purity" (1 Tim 5.1b–2 *NIV*). If this helps in what Jennifer Slater calls "The Catholic Church in need of de-clericalisation," (Slater 2019), then it is worth it. When I was ordained on 14 August 1983, I had a human-spiritual whisperer in my bishop, the late Dennis Harold de Jong. Sadly, they never make them like him anymore.

5. The Human-Spiritual Whisperer from the ends of the Earth

Priestly formation is about human whispering — the fostering of our understanding of others, and to use that understanding to unlock our persuasive abilities and exert influence in a non-manipulative way so as to get the most out of their human potential. All of us were created for a unique contribution to humanity and human-spiritual whisperers help to sniff that out of us. The best chance, now and in the near future for this to happen in the Catholic Church is the bishop of Rome from the ends of the earth who took a papal name, hitherto not tried for size, unlike his predecessors, Francis. He is our papal human-spiritual whisperer in the make of a John XXIII and a John Paul I, calling us to be human-spiritual whisperers to each other. Luckily, on a global stage, that all changed on 13 March 2013 when the universal Church was gifted a global human-spiritual whisperer.

Initial Seminary formation was practically on the tip of Pope Francis' tongue soon after his election as Pope on that drizzly 13 March 2013 Rome evening when he introduced himself to the city and to the world — *Urbi et Orbi*: "Brothers and sisters, good evening! You all know that the duty of the Conclave was to give Rome a bishop. It seems that my brother cardinals have gone almost to the ends of the earth to get him [*Fratelli e sorelle, buonasera! Voi sapete che il dovere del Conclave era di dare un vescovo a Roma. Sembra che i miei fratelli cardinali siano andati a prenderlo quasi alla fine del mondo*].[23] He was our brother, not the Holy Father, a title I suspect he finds difficult to wear. Eight months later, the Pope referred to poor priestly formation that leads to the creation of "little monsters" [*piccoli mostri*] not so much as a criticism of candidates for the priesthood *in se* but as a criticism of the broken system that produced them and nurtured them. On 29 November 2013, He spoke to 120 superiors of religious orders during a closed-door meeting where he expressed his disquiet with seminary formation.

> If the seminary is too large, it must be divided into communities with formators capable of truly accompanying people. Dialogue must be serious, fearless, and sincere. And we must consider that the language of young people in formation today is different from that of those who preceded them: we are living in a changed epoch. Training is a work of art, not policing. We must form the heart. Otherwise we form little monsters. And then these little monsters form the people of God. This really gives me goosebumps [*Se il seminario è troppo grande, bisogna dividerlo in comunità con formatori capaci di seguire davvero le persone. Il dialogo deve essere serio, senza paura, sincero. E bisogna considerare che il linguaggio dei giovani in formazione oggi è diverso da quello di chi li ha preceduti: viviamo un cambiamento d'epoca. La formazione è un'opera artigianale, non poliziesca. Dobbiamo formare il cuore. Altrimenti formiamo piccoli mostri. E poi questi piccoli mostri formano il popolo di Dio. Questo mi fa venire davvero la pelle d'oca*].[24]

Bill McGarvey, writing for *America the Jesuit Review* confirms that during that meeting the Pope registered disappointment, telling his audience that seminary formation must be "a work of art, not a police action" where seminarians "grit their teeth, try not to make mistakes, follow the rules smiling a lot, just waiting for the day when they are told 'Good, you have finished [your] formation.'"[25]

6. Little Monsters Look Like This

I wonder what Pope Francis meant by little monsters. I have scoured his writings since that famous locution and I am still none the wiser. So, I decided to come up with the category: little monsters look like this and I found that description in a book by Richard Gula, *Just Ministry: Professional Ethics for Pastoral Ministers* (2010) from which I will cite generously presently.

> We are not fit for ministry if we cannot relate — that is, if we show no signs of having sustained friendships, are careless about boundaries, are arrogant or quarrelsome, or if our style of relating is to control, intimidate, exploit, manipulate, demean, or shame. Nor should anyone be a candidate for ministry who is ideologically or emotionally rigid, aloof, passive, defensive, argumentative, authoritarian, selfish, dismissive, or resistant to learning.
>
> Rather, we ought to manifest a fundamental openness to people and ideas, be hospitable and affable, non-defensive, flexible, capable of collaborating, compassionate, desiring justice, and able to move beyond our own interests in order to be ready to serve others. From my years of experience in seminary formation, I have concluded that seminarians come to the seminary with their relational habits well in place. The seminary cannot do much to get seminarians to acquire the habits needed to have life-giving, satisfying, supportive relationships. Consequently, the diocese should not accept candidates who have not already manifested a history of healthy relationships (Gula 2010: 13–14).

Little and big ecclesiastical monsters are the exact opposite of "hospitable and affable, non-defensive, flexible, capable of collaborating, compassionate, desiring justice, and able to move beyond our own interests in order to be ready to serve others." They are dismissive of boundaries, are arrogant and quarrelsome. They are anal retentive and want to be in control all the time. Patriarchy and clericalism give them the licence to manipulate, demean or shame. They are ideologically fixated, aloof, defensive and generally resistant to the signs of the times. Recently, I came across one such unfortunate. He is an American priest who became famous by spouting and pontificating that an American Catholic could not be Catholic and vote democratic[26] just before the recent American Presidential elections. His name is James Altman, currently pastor of St James the Less Catholic Church of the diocese of La Crosse. His pontificating was aired by an outfit called, Alpha News. It added the blurb, "Father James Altman calls out the hypocrisies of Church hierarchy and their destructive leftist politicization of the Catholic Church that has slapped faithful Catholics in the face and led many others astray. Altman also explains the basis of human nature and our purpose in life."[27] Wisely, his bishop, William Callahan of La Crosse said in a 9 September statement that "Canon law indicates that before penalties are imposed, we need to ensure that fraternal correction, rebuke or other means of pastoral solicitude will not be sufficient to repair the scandal,"[28] the bishop added, in reference to canon 1341 of the Church's Code of Canon Law.

7. An oft-broken System still capable of turning out Masterpieces

In the light of my broken system record, where seminarians lived every day in fear of expulsion for not "following the rules a lot" it is a miracle that some of them still turned out well-formed. Simon Kalolo Kabanda for instance, went on to become a priest a *kopala* [Copperbelt] priest, after serving out a 2-year suspension for being a ring-leader in the May 1985 seminary boycott. He was brought up on the Gospel of emancipation with a big social conscience for the poor and downtrodden, a conscience he has carried into his passion as a Constitution educator, including the process of coming up with a people-centred Constitution. At that November meeting of the Pope and Religious superiors, Pope Francis went on to unmask the hypocrisy inherent in a "grit your teeth or smile a lot" formation which he described as the result of "clericalism, which is one of the worst evils." For the Pope, priestly formation "must form their hearts. Otherwise we are creating little monsters. And then these little monsters mould the people of God. This really gives me goose bumps."[29]

At the end of the day, I am not sure how many Zambian bishops, when they receive the seminary reports from the rectors of Emmaus Spirituality Centre, *Mpima* Major Seminary and St Dominic's Major seminary are getting any goose bumps on account of future little monsters. I was extremely fortunate to have a bishop of the heart and stature of Dennis Harold de Jong. When he had read a good spiritual book, he often kept a copy for me. During the 1990s he complained to me that he had ordained far too many pagans. The Pope would say, we are breeding too many little monsters. I suspect most of my current bishops' main worry is the bottom line and how to meet the deficit after the subsidy from Rome and the contributions from the parishes have been added up and to confirm various appointments in the diocese on the basis of reward and punishment. In one particular case, the recent death of my friend, bishop Justin Mulenga who was the director of seminaries needed someone like him to take his place. He was one of life's good men gone too soon but I doubt if his replacement was a human-spiritual whisperer as he was.

8. An Italian Professor and the oft-Broken System

Just to give a bit of background to how broken the system of priestly formation is, you will need the benefit of time travel, not to the future, I am afraid, but back to the past and specifically to 1563. I like to concretise events in terms of historical time. In the history of Catholicism, 1563 marked the end of the Council of Trent and the beginning of what we have come to know as priestly formation, 457 years ago. If this does not spook you, nothing I say after this, will. Since almost 500 years ago, that is half-a-century ago when priestly formation started, very little has changed of substance. This could be a plus. Tried and tested. But often a minus. Broken and anachronistic. It is a matter of "As it was in the beginning, is now and ever shall be, the world without end." Human institutions just do work like that. Professor Alberto Melloni of the John XXII *Foundation for Religious Sciences* (Bologna, Italy) recently pointed out that the archetype of today's priest dates back to over 400 years ago and the reforms stemming from the Council of

Trent (1545–1563). The university professor pointed this out in a 22 March 2017 article for the Rome-based daily, *La Repubblica*.

> In the background, a great cycle has ended: that of the priest. That formidable sixteenth-century invention that shaped the culture and politics, psychology and interior life, art and theology of the West and its ancient colonies did not become extinct (there are about 420 thousand priests in the world), but for over a century it is in a crisis (my translation) [*In sordina, si è esaurito un grande ciclo: quello del prete. Quella formidabile invenzione cinquecentesca che ha plasmato la cultura e la politica, la psicologia e la vita interiore, l'arte e la teologia dell' Occidente e delle sue antiche colonie non si è estinta (sono circa 420 mila i preti nel mondo), ma da oltre un secolo è in crisi*].[30]

For once we are in agreement with the Council of Trent's aim of priestly formation as "*cura animarum*." What we disagree on is the means of getting there. There was a time, as one of the few major benefits of the role of the priest arising from the Tridentine Council, the role of the priest as "*cura animarum*" [care of souls] was straightforward. What the Catholic priest today takes for granted was quite a novelty at the Council of Trent, especially training and formation. It is this novelty that needs re-inventing, particularly how to achieve that. This is how an Italian author, Angelo Turchini, characterises the end product.

> The parish, guided by the pastor, developed as a centre of sacramental life as well as a place for the daily management of the sacred, but also a registry, assistance centre, a pivot of spiritual life. The time during which the clergy, especially in the rural areas, were completely incapable of administering confession and providing basic catechesis, was long gone [*La parrocchia, guidata dal parroco, diventa centro di vita sacra mentale e luogo della quotidiana gestione del sacro, ma anche anagrafe, centro di assistenza, perno di vita spirituale. Il tempo in cui il clero, specie nelle zone rurali, era totalmente incapace di confessare e di impartire la catechesi di base, è lontano*] (Turchini 1995: 235).

But today, there is a dazzling array of providers of "*cura animarum*" [care of souls] in droves, from psychiatrists, psychotherapists, psychologists, and even quacks, charlatans, fortune tellers and shamans to double-breasted and jet flying pastors from *Deeper Penetration Ministries*, apostles and prophets, counsellors after three weeks' psycho-social Counselling from *Kara Counselling Trust*, even salesmen of retail therapy, traditional healers from the Democratic Republic of the Congo or *Mununga* and latter-day slayers in the spirit. The Catholic priest's merchandise monopoly is no more. The result is not far from what I have described as spiritually spoiled brats or Pope Francis' little monsters who join the above ranks, because "if you can't beat them, join them." These "little monsters" then become "huge monsters" when they are appointed diocesan treasurers, vicar-generals, Judicial vicars, Monsignors, bishops and archbishops and the production machinery continues. Alberto Melloni calls the result "clericalism."

> The loss of role and emotional neglect exposes him [the priest] to the worst: up to the slavish exaltation of celibacy that traps sexuality in search of sublimation and attracts unresolved or even sick people to the priesthood. His qualification becomes the name of a vice that has never been fought sufficiently: clericalism [*La perdita di ruolo e l'incuria affettiva lo espone al peggio: fino alla svenevole esaltazione del celibato che intrappola la sessualità in cerca di sublimazione e attira nel presbiterato persone irrisolte o addirittura malate. La sua qualifica diventa il nome di un vizio mai combattuto abbastanza: il clericalismo*] (*Ibid*).

The above picture was thrown into stark relief by the recent searingly honest *McCarrick Report* into the sexual abuse scandal generated by high profile former Cardinal Archbishop of Washington, Theodore McCarrick (*McCarrick Report* 2020). Elsewhere, I argue that the *McCarrick Report* is a sign of a dysfunctional system held together by clericalism, patriarchy, secrecy and sovereignty. Sexual abuse in the Catholic Church will not be rooted out unless the two twin villains of clericalism and patriarchy, secrecy and sovereignty are thrown out of the tent. In terms of its hierarchy, it needs to reflect the rest of society comprising male and female, straight and gay, married and celibate, young and old (Mukuka 2020 b). On the upside, As John Allen says, "In the end, it's possible the *McCarrick Report* may be remembered as the single most consequential step toward reform during the Francis papacy, not only because of what it reveals about this particular case, but the precedent it sets for how all future cases ought to be handled. Once the genie of transparency is out of the bottle, that is, it's going to be awfully difficult to put it back in."[31] It is hoped that two of the corollaries of the *McCarrick Report* should lead to a change in the way bishops are vetted, selected and appointed in the Catholic and the way candidates to the priesthood are selected, vetted, accompanied and mentored. Bishops ought to be elected by their constituency to a limited or even to a lower retirement age of 65 or whichever comes first (Mukuka 2020b). Candidates to the priesthood need an open and transparent system in which they can be humanly-spiritually whispered into fully human and fully alive disciples of the Palestinian Rabbi.

9. But Why is Clericalism such a *bête noire*?

To play the devil's advocate, it may be argued that what we are characterising as clericalism is what has kept the priesthood and the institutional Church together. If it isn't broken, why fix it? That's just the point, it is broken. All you need is a few hours of the *McCarrick Report* to change your mind. Jennifer Slater is right to point out that "Clericalism is directly linked to seminary formation towards the office of priesthood whereby candidates precipitously perceive themselves as distinct from the 'faithful' or the 'laity' in whose pastoral service they are meant to be" (Slater 2019). Just so that we are on the same page, what is clericalism and why is it such a *bête noire*? I think Russell Shaw answers both questions adequately.

By "clericalism" I mean an elitist mindset, together with structures and patterns of behaviour corresponding to it, which takes it for granted that clerics — in the Catholic context, mainly bishops and priests — are intrinsically superior to the other members of the Church and deserve automatic deference. Passivity and dependency are the laity's lot. By no means is clericalism confined to clerics themselves. The clericalist mindset is widely shared by the Catholic lay people (Shaw 2008: 15).

I think this elitist mindset must go back at least as far back as patriarchal religion, when men appropriated the original worship of earth mother goddess. As Cynthia Eller points out, "The new male ruling class that ushered in the patriarchy is generally understood to have been a group of invaders from the North Eurasian steppes who imposed a patrilineal kinship system and male deities on the Goddess-worshiping cultures" (Eller 1991: 285). Janet Michello links this change to the under-acknowledgement of African Traditional Religion. She argues that "one reason for the important role of African folk religion being under-acknowledged is because the strength of female power is a threat to religious patriarchy" (Michello 2020: 7). The ensuing specialisation in the cult by men began to be used as an instrument of wresting power from women. This could easily have taken place already some two thousand years before the birth of Jesus Christ. In an earlier article showing the link between clericalism and the sex abuse scandal, Russell Shaw was right to opine that

> Clericalism in the Catholic Church is something like the pattern in the wallpaper: it's been there so long you don't see it anymore. That may be why, amid all the demands for change in response to the scandal of clergy sex abuse, more has not been heard about clericalism and the need to get rid of it once and for all. Yet clericalism and the clericalist culture are at the heart of this noxious episode.[32]

I am interested in the above quotation from the clericalism angle but I do take the point that "when sex abuse occurs in a clericalist context, as in the case of Theodore McCarrick, the situation takes on a distinctively clericalist coloration that makes matters worse."[33] In Africa, rather than child sex abuse, our Achilles Heel is sexual abuse of women, including nuns being forced to abort. Jesus Christ found and fought religious clericalism. He was realistic enough that he was not going to dismantle it in one day and counselled his followers to do what the religious leaders say rather than follow what they do.

> **23** Then Jesus said to the crowds and to his disciples, ² 'The Scribes and the Pharisees sit on Moses' seat; ³ therefore, do whatever they teach you and follow it; but do not do as they do, for they do not practise what they teach. ⁴ They tie up heavy burdens, hard to bear, and lay them on the shoulders of others; but they themselves are unwilling to lift a finger to move them. ⁵ They do all their deeds to be seen by others; for they make their phylacteries broad and their fringes

long. ⁶ They love to have the place of honour at banquets and the best seats in the synagogues, ⁷ and to be greeted with respect in the market-places, and to have people call them rabbi. ⁸ But you are not to be called rabbi, for you have one teacher, and you are all students. ⁹ And call no one your father on earth, for you have one Father —the one in heaven. ¹⁰ Nor are you to be called instructors, for you have one instructor, the Messiah. ¹¹ The greatest among you will be your servant. ¹² All who exalt themselves will be humbled, and all who humble themselves will be exalted (Mt 23.112 *NRSV*).

Sadly, two thousand years after the ministry of the Palestinian Rabbi, religious clericalism is still alive and well and we are still calling others Rabbi, father or instructor in that exclusive sense that only belongs to God. Clericalism is ultimately the deification of one's fellow human beings and is the point Jesus is making by proscribing calling any human being Rabbi, father or instructor. In the ultimate spiritual and religious sense, only God is our true Rabbi, father and instructor. This deification is promoted by both clerics and laity such as the lay Catholic manager of the Shoprite Supermarket in my home town Ndola who sent one of his minions to facilitate my jumping the queue, much to the displeasure of other shoppers who had been languishing in the queue longer than me. He added that if I needed anything, all I needed to do was phone. Rather than educate him on the evils of religious clericalism as deification of one's fellow human beings, I took the easy way out and shopped elsewhere where my clerical honour was not immediately visible. Just as well, although I was Ndola-brought up, I had never plied my trade in the town long enough to be identified everywhere. Why lay people would promote clericalism is anybody's guess. My guess is vicarious enjoyment. The laity have convinced themselves that the priesthood was the equivalent of rubbing shoulders with religious celebrities. What you cannot enjoy directly, you might as well enjoy by association, especially family members who introduced themselves as the brother or sister of the priest. It was as if the honour of the priesthood had rubbed off on them by some process of spiritual osmosis communicated via a common gene pool. In turn, such unfortunate souls also got the clerical class A treatment. Part of my father's resistance to my quitting the ministerial priesthood was the loss of honour and subsequent shame of the collateral damage of the father of an ex-priest. Whatever sheen my family had enjoyed for 14 years was now coming off. Clericalism is so wrong that one wonders why it has survived for so long. But may be that should not be surprising.

> In a special way, however, clericalism is rooted in the idea that in whatever pertains to religion, it is the right and the responsibility of clerics to make the decisions and give the orders, and the job of lay people to carry them out. At a deep level it is spiritual snobbery reflecting the assumption that the clerical state in and of itself makes clerics spiritually superior to the laity. A mistaken idea of vocation is at work here — the idea that the calling to ordained ministry is superior to all other vocations.[34]

Priestly formation since the end of the Council of Trent in 1563 has failed to root out clericalism. In fact, it has been nourished by it. Most beneficiaries do not have the appetite for a new menu to replace clericalism. The payoff must be high and part of the reason is that it is the cheapest way to get, use and abuse power while maintaining a fairly high status, especially one nurtured by hard power. Soft power takes too much cajoling and convincing. If the bishop says jump, for instance, the question is not, why but how high my Lord? One former colleague, now gone back to his reward, began to believe that God-given powers to bring people back from the dead. In any other walk of life, he should have been sectioned.

10. Priestly Formation as Artisanal

This section is my *crux interpretum*. I broach the question, "How can we make formation of candidates to the priesthood, and indeed to other vocations including married life more artisanal? I was involved in priestly formation for 7 years out of my 14 years in my Catholic ministerial priesthood. If you take out 4 years of graduate studies, one and half of leave of absence, it leaves me only one and half of parish ministry, 6 months of which I spent preparing for the visit of Pope John Paul II to Kitwe on 5 May 1989 sliding from one committee meeting to another. With these timelines, I want to underscore my passion for priestly formation. As my former student, Eugene Nyambe tells me 35 years later, "I still think you have that deep concern and passion for formation" (email, 23 June 2020).

I am grateful for this affirmation but I am not sure that my "deep concern and passion for formation" was coming from the right place, the heart. If I have learnt anything about myself in various counselling courses I have done over the years, it is that my emotional intelligence and rational intelligence did not always communicate to each other. I often let my rational intelligence do the talking. Contrary to what most people believe that their opinions, moral decisions or even political opinions are the result of reason, sadly or in actual fact they are all the result of emotional investment. Once that investment has been made, reason is then drafted in to justify the investment. Otherwise, there is no way to explain how after 4 years of Donald Trump, 70 million Americans still think he is the right man to "Make America Great Again." Having what my own formators convinced me was a very high IQ, I believed that formation was a matter of reason and logic — a work of science. I now realise it is a matter of the heart — a work of art and most of the time the recommendation that a candidate cannot be promoted to holy orders is a hunch rather than a certainty. Our candidates, rightly or wrongly feel that they cannot be kicked out on a hunch. They invent a reasonable explanation that is not true or one that they can think their mates can believe. Only a human-spiritual whisperer can communicate a hunch.

If I am being honest, the model of formation I underwent as a seminarian, especially at *Mpima* Major Seminary (1976–1979) and later participated in as a formator (1983–1987 and 1993–1995) was a prison or policing model guided by reason and sometimes the lack of it. Appropriately, the very first subject we introduced to the first-year seminarian was logic. We contradicted ourselves by telling our students that vocation is a matter of faith or the heart but proceeded to try to reason it out and impressed on the student St Anselm's axiom, *fides quaerens intellectum* [faith seeking understanding]. While *fides quaerens intellectum* made sense at one level, it was the *intellectus quaerens fidem* [intelligence seeking faith] dog whistle we were playing. I am happy for any of my co-formators to beg to differ but it was still my experience.

At least six of my co-formators have gone back to the Lord: my uncle, Alex Chanda, Jude Rochford (my rector twice — as a seminarian and as a formator), Karl Hannecart (as former teacher and colleague), Jack O'Leary, Normand Papineau and Johannes Tappeser (as former teacher and colleague). One of the issues that has come to the surface in my taking stock of the 1985 seminary boycott is that students lived in a climate of fear. Two images come to mind. They were like petty criminals who had re-offended and any time they would be arrested and if convicted, they would be sent for penal or corrective incarceration. Ironically, they feared being paroled and sent back home. An ex-prisoner was never a welcome stigma for the ex-seminarian. The result was that whatever petty crime they had committed in a previous life or in the present — that baggage of hurt or dysfunction I talked about above — and it was mainly to do with the exercise of their virile member for other than urinary purposes, silence and amnesia were the best policy.

The photo was removed by the editors for copyright reasons.

Friar Jude Rochford Ofm Conv, one of the pioneers who opened *Mpima* Major Seminary in 1973. He was the third rector after Killian Speckner and David Cullen [Photo credit: Conventual Franciscan Friars, Province of Our Lady of Consolation, Mount St. Francis, Indiana].

11. How an Irish Priest was not well-served by a Dysfunctional System

An example of this policy was a young Irish priest I knew in the 1970s. He always struck me as odd. He never liked girls or women. Long after I had left the ministerial priesthood, I sought him out and we met at London's Marylebone station over a cup of Starbucks coffee. His missionary organisation had let him go for deciding to come out of the gay closet. We quickly exchanged pleasantries and he proceeded to fill me in. As an 18-year-old seminarian at Maynooth in the mid-1960s, he approached his spiritual director wondering whether he was gay or not. The spiritual director strongly upbraided him and told him if he wanted to be a priest, he was never to speak about this. After his first Zambian tour of duty, he left for graduate and postgraduate studies to the USA where he came out as being gay while pursuing a doctorate in Counselling. My friend still considers himself a priest, a married one to boot. His husband is a psychotherapist. He had never been allowed to as much as confess or explore his "sin." There is an ironic twist to his priestly "sin." While living in the United States, he received a trans-Atlantic telephone call from his seminary ex- spiritual director who was now retired as a priest and living in London. He wanted to visit his former student. They met in New York. My friend's former spiritual director wanted to apologise. He too was gay and needed help coming out. The bottom line is that both were victims of a policing or prison model of priestly formation.

Many of my informants for this article can vouchsafe for the policing or prison model of formation. The two immediate triggers of the boycott are symptomatic of a police force or prison service at its best. 13 students were fired for making girls pregnant in what can only have been a procreative epidemic in February 1985. They were fired to prevent them spreading a new strain of the age-old procreative virus — a sort of *procreationis virus* [*provid*-85] — further, in order to facilitate contact tracing and controlling the spread of the virus which as yet had no known vaccine and so far, had been resistant to cold showers, prayer and fasting. On 17 May 1985, Swithan Kalobwe followed suite. He was given matching orders shortly before he was due to graduate with a Diploma in Philosophy and Religious Studies. The official reason given by the rector was the same *provid*-85 after allegedly testing positive but by his own testimony, it was an intercepted acceptance letter from the University of Zambia by the missionary police or prison warder. He was immediately isolated, quarantined and sent home. This was the match that lit the powder keg. You be the judge whether this policing or prison model of formation was fit for the purpose of evangelical empowerment driven by the Nazareth *Manifesto*. Later, I suggest an alternative model.

12. In the Meantime, Clericalism Keeps Repeating Itself

History keeps repeating itself. The Church claims to empower with the Gospel. I will cite a recent example that shows that sometimes we do the reverse. Our abuse of power in 1985 in an African seminary is not atypical as the following news item shows, largely showing the official side of the story.

> The Vatican has appointed a commission headed by an apostolic delegate to revise the statutes and directorate of the lay association *Memores Domini* — consecrated lay faithful who are part of the Communion and Liberation movement. At a June 26 meeting with *Memores Domini* leaders, Cardinal Kevin Farrell, the prefect of the Dicastery for Laity, Family and Life, appointed Jesuit Father Gianfranco Ghirlanda, a specialist in canon law, as the apostolic delegate to oversee the process, according to Italian journalist Aldo Maria Valli who confirmed the news. The story was first reported on June 26 by the Italian blog *Messainlatino*.[35]

But as everyone knows, it takes two to tangle. The above story was first reported by the Italian blog *Messainlatino*, which gives a different spin that all is not well in that patch of God's flock and that we may be dealing with a bigger fish to fry here: ecclesiastical (read clerical) versus lay power and your guess is probably the same as mine who is going to win.

> *Nostre fonti interne ci riferiscono che l'organizzazione dei consacrati laici di CL [Communione e Liberazione], i Memores Domini, sia stata commissariata. E'*

da tempo che la dirigenza di CL, Julián Carrón in testa, è in polemica con la maggioranza dei Memores che rivendicano la loro autonomia laicale. Sembra che sia stato richiesto l'aiuto di Roma e, invece, sarebbe arrivato il commissariamento dell'associazione, con la gestione di tutta l'operazione da parte del controverso Prefetto del Dicastero per i laici, la famiglia e la vita, il card. Kevin Farrell. Il Commissario nominato sarebbe padre Gianfranco Ghirlanda, gesuita, già assistente ai commissariati Legionari di Cristo. Anche se formalmente potrebbe essere un responsabile per la revisione degli statuti. Tra le voci che girano c'è anche la nomina ad arcivescovo di Julián Carrón stesso, con un incarico curiale, e il passaggio, a capo di CL, ad un altro personaggio ugualmente di gradimento del S. Padre Francesco[36] [Our internal sources report that the organisation of lay consecrated persons of CL (Communion and Liberation), the *Memores Domini*, has been placed under a commission. CL's leadership, Julián Carrón as head, has long been in controversy with the majority of *Memores* who claim their lay autonomy. It seems that the help of Rome was requested and, instead, the placement of the association under a commission would arrive, with the management of the whole operation under the controversial Prefect of the Dicastery for the laity, family and life, card. Kevin Farrell. The nominated Commissioner would be Father Gianfranco Ghirlanda, a Jesuit, formerly, assistant to the Legionary Commissariat of Christ. Although formally he would be responsible for the revision of the statutes. Among the rumours doing the rounds, there is also the appointment as archbishop of Julián Carrón himself, with a curial assignment, and the passing on, at the head of CL, to another person, equally pleasing to the Holy Father Francis].

I don't know Julián Carrón from Adam but he strikes me as being on the conservative end of the conservative-liberal spectrum. One way I would imagine to get into the mind of Julián Carrón is to read his 2017 book, *Disarming Beauty: Essays on Faith, Truth and Freedom*. Reading between the lines, *Communione e Liberazione* [official name, *Fraternità di Communione e Liberazione* — Fraternity of Communion and Liberation] seems to be a brainchild of Pope Benedict XVI, although founded by an Italian priest, Luigi Giovanni Giussani in 1954. It appears to be an association that ticks the emeritus Pope's agenda. Some of this agenda was hinted at when Pope Benedict XVI granted an audience to CL in 2007. He reminded CL that still today, it "offers a profound way of life and actualizes the Christian faith, both in total fidelity and communion with the Successor of Peter and with the Pastors who assure the governing of the Church and through spontaneity and freedom permit new and prophetic, apostolic and missionary achievements" (Benedict XVI, Audience with CL, 24 March 2007).[37]

Pope Francis, rightly or wrongly wants to flex his papal muscle and leave his own imprint on the organisation. Whatever the Pope's intentions are, I hope that the newly appointed commissioner will take the likes of Zita V Tóth's scathing critique of the group into account.

> All in all, while the name of CL [Communion and Liberation] suggests that they aim at building community (communion) and freedom (liberation), they achieve neither — and with the current structure of the organization, this failure is not accidental. They cannot achieve communion since every part of the organization is controlled in a totalitarian way, resulting in a disenfranchised community. They cannot achieve liberation since there is no freedom where there is no thinking.[38]

There is something raw and undigested about Zita Tóth's critique of CL which I find unphilosophical and unbalanced. She does not have a good word to say about CL. So, I am taking it with a pinch of salt. My problem goes back to the beginning. The organisation was founded by a celibate priest. There does seem to be something paternalistic and inherently patriarchal in their exercise of power. When the founder Luigi Giovanni Giussani died in 2005, there was an opportunity to place CL under lay leadership which was passed up with the appointment of Julián Carrón, another celibate priest, presumably appointed by the Vatican. There was always going to be a tug of war between the pro-clerical and pro-laity camps within CL. Whatever Pope Francis' intentions are, he is faced with a catch-22 situation: If he appoints another priestly head of CL, he is playing into maintaining ecclesiastical power supremacy which is the source of the problem in the first place. If he appoints a lay head, he risks affronting his predecessor who lives a stone throw from his residence. Whether Pope Francis caves in again to hard power, it won't be the first time. Most people expected him to consider the ordination of *viri probati* after the Amazon synod until Benedict XVI and Robert Sarah's *From the bottom of our hearts* (2020) put the spanner in the works. And if the truth be told, hard power is not caring power, which in reference to formation, Pope Francis seems to be encouraging. As a researcher I have attempted to hear from the horse's mouth by writing to CL. I am not putting too any eggs in that basket for a response.

> *Sono un accademico dello Zambia che sta facendo sul potere duro (hard power) e morbido (soft) nella Chiesa Cattolica. Mi chiedo se potrei ottenere il parere di CL sulla nomina di un commissario per esaminare il rinnovo dello statuto di CL. C'è qualcosa di rotto che il Santo Padre vuole riparare in CL? Il blog Messainlatino sembra implicare che ci sono due campi in CL: quelli pro- Julián Carrón e quelli contra. Infine, se si dice che Julián Carrón potrebbe essere un arcivesco, quale sarebbe la preferenza di CL tra la direzione priestlye o laica.. Vi ringrazio in anticipo per l'aiuto* [I am a Zambian academic researching use of hard power and soft power in the Catholic Church. May I ask for your opinion regarding the appointment of a commissioner to look into the renewal of statutes of CL? Is there something broken in CL which the Holy

Father want fixed? The blog *Messainlatino* seems to imply that there are two camps in CL: the pro and contra Julián Carrón. Finally, there is word that Julián Carrón may be up for an archbishopric, what would be the preference of CL between a clerical or lay direction? Thanking you in anticipation for your assistance] (email sent 8 July 2020).

13. The Human-Spiritual Whisperer and Accompaniment

I aver that there is always an alternative model to hard power, what I have referred to as the prison or policing model, especially in the context of priestly formation — a caring model. Pope Francis has described it as formation as "a work art" [*un opera artigianale*]. Sister Maryasia Weber, a Religious Sister of Mercy, a physician and Psychiatrist has ably described this formation in her book, *The Art of Accompaniment: Practical Steps for the Seminary Formator* (2018). According to her, the role of a seminary formator is to accompany the seminarian in the external forum and to discern with him and hopefully in the near future her, the seminary community [students and staff, including and especially kitchen staff — after all, we are what we eat], and larger Church community, to which I would specify the small Christian community of origin, parish and diocese in that order, whether the candidate has a specific vocation to the Catholic ministerial priesthood or other ministries within the Church exercising the priesthood of the people of God. She argues that to accomplish this task effectively, the formator needs to be able to multitask using a robust toolkit of skills that will enable him or her to listen, understand, encourage, challenge, and adequately assess the seminarian in an open and honest way. I was not convinced that this could be done by the academic lecturer primarily. It needed a professional human and spiritual whisperer and the closest I came to one in my 7 years was Jack O'Leary. His type of formation was an art and not a science, akin to human whispering. The model best suited to accomplish this in my view is the ancient *cura animarum* model or the Bergoglian "formation as an art model." In chapter two of her book, clearly for me her *pièce de résistance*, Sister Maryasia Weber discusses "Markers of human maturation in seminary formation: becoming a gift for others" (Weber 2018: 33–54).

I think the six markers of human maturation ought to be available to every teenager as they transition from teenage hood to adulthood when they move from secondary school to tertiary education. Instead of having a director of vocations, dioceses should consider a broader office of Episcopal Vicar for Accompaniment and Discernment in view of vocations to the married life and celibate life — whether as lay people, diocesan priests or religious life.

14. Markers of human maturation in seminary formation

Citing two important documents, *Guidelines for the use of Psychology in the admission and formation of seminarians for the priesthood* (2008) and the *Ratio Fundamentalis Institutionis Sacerdotalis* (2016), Sister Maryasia Weber lists six markers by which to evaluate whether a candidate for holy orders has matured sufficiently to present himself for ordination: self-knowledge, self-direction, self-control, self-discipline, self-governance and spiritual fatherhood [and motherhood] (Weber 2018: 33–56 and 75–85).[39] And quite frankly these are markers of human maturation I would be looking for in anyone planning to marry or to stay celibate even for non-religious reasons and a big argument why the current *cura animarum* offered to seminarians ought to be opened up to a wider clientele. I am just surprised that, written in 2018, *The Art of Accompaniment: Practical Steps for the Seminary Formator* does not include spiritual motherhood, especially for male candidates. Sister Maryasia Weber breaks down the markers of human maturation as follows.

> Cited among the virtues and abilities in a priest are a positive and stable sense of his masculine [and feminine] identity, the capacity to form mature relationships, a solid sense of belonging, self-knowledge, the capacity for self-correction, the ability for trust and loyalty, and the courage to stay faithful to decisions made before God (Weber 2018: 34).

Although the Catholic Church does not yet admit women to ordination, most studies show how admitting women to the priesthood will give it a balance it lacks. But that is a Pandora's Box for another day. Suffice it to say, with Pamela Cooper-White, that "Women's advent into ordained leadership has the potential for shifting more than just ecclesial power structures. The relatively sudden juxtaposition of metaphors of birth with the actual enfleshed experiences of birthing in the persons of the Church's ministers may well impact some of the Church's deepest rituals and the ways in which Christianity's deepest symbols may now be received by believers."[40]

The key to the six markers is the little word "self" and just as well self-knowledge comes first. The Ancient Greeks had an aphorism to that effect, "know thyself" [Greek: γνῶθι σεαυτόν]. It was one of the Delphic maxims and was the first of three maxims inscribed in the forecourt of the Temple of Apollo at Delphi [ancient sanctuary and seat of Pythia — the high priestess of the Temple]. In 1734, the English poet Alexander Pope wrote a poem entitled "An Essay on Man, Epistle II" which begins "Know then thyself, presume not God to scan, the proper study of mankind is man."[41] This cardinal Delphic maxim inserts itself quite comfortably in another maxim attributed to Socrates at his trial, "The unexamined life is not worth living" [ὁ ἀνεξέταστος βίος οὐ βιωτὸς ἀνθρώπῳ]. Julian Baggini explains this maxim as follows.

> The ideal of the examined life is noble for precisely this reason. It sounds unobjectionable: an encouragement to be fully human, to use our highly developed faculty of thought to raise our existence above that of mere beasts. For if we don't think, we are no more than animals, simply eating, sleeping, working and procreating. And though it may be a bit strong to say such lives are not worth living, all but a minority of ethical vegetarians would agree that they are much less valuable than fully human ones.[42]

For Socrates, an examined life was the pursuit of the love of wisdom, of philosophy. Socrates chose to die rather than to be exiled to some godforsaken island where he would not be able to pursue this life, to philosophise. As he says in his own words, while waiting to be killed for polluting the mind of Athenian youth, presumably on account of his philosophical teachings. "Perhaps someone might say, 'Socrates, can you not go away from us and live quietly, without talking?' Now this is the hardest thing to make some of you believe. For if I say that such conduct would be disobedience to the god and that therefore I cannot keep quiet, you will think I am jesting and will not believe me; And if again I say that to talk every day about virtue and the other things about which you hear me talking and examining myself and others is the greatest good to man, and that the unexamined life is not worth living, you will believe me still less. This is as I say, gentlemen, but it is not easy to convince you. Besides, I am not accustomed to think that I deserve anything bad as large as I could pay; for that would have done me no harm. But as it is — I have no money, unless you are willing to impose a fine which I could pay" (Plato, *Apologia*, 37e–38b).[43]

The class of 1985 who were involved in the seminary boycott loved Socrates and Plato. I thought the above reminder will jog their memories quite nicely. Since Sister Maryasia Weber is quoting or paraphrasing the *Guidelines* and the *Ratio* above, I can understand the "sexist" language but I think that is unfortunate. Although she first came up with these markers in 2009, you would think by 2018, the author would have airbrushed "sense of his masculine identity" and "spiritual fatherhood" as I have done in her list. This is what I understood when I was signing up for, minus for obvious reasons, the missing female component, when my friend Joe Komakoma drove me to take up my appointment on Friday, 22 August 1983 at *Mpima* Major Seminary as a formator. Instead, I run into an all-male formation police and warder system and became complicit. My teenage temper tantrums each time we voted to expel a student on any markers of human maturation we ourselves were far from realising were never known to the students. For most of the students, I was the young smiling assassin spying for the enemy and couriering enemy intelligence to the staff. For the staff, I was the young and naive avuncular students' megaphone. I was caught up between the devil and the deep blue sea.

15. Devolving Papal Power to Episcopal Conferences Still a Pie in the Sky

Papal devolution of power is still a pie in the sky, despite the best intentions of Pope Francis. Alberto Melloni's analysis of the priesthood ends on a semi hopeful note but it requires those Pope Francis wants to share power with to take it but it appears they lack the will or the strength to do so. It is even possible that it is the Pope not letting go of centuries' old power and authority such as Pope Francis tried to exercise in the standoff with the Nigerian diocese of *Ahiara* in Southeastern Nigeria until he blinked.

> On the other hand, the most significant decision of the pontificate [of Francis], the one contained in *Evangelii Gaudium*, has not yet been accepted by the bishops: it is the one that states that episcopal conferences have "authentic doctrinal authority." It would therefore be up to the local ordinaries to raise a theme on which the life of their Churches is at stake: but indolence prevails,

encouraged by the hope that tomorrow's reform will have the same courage as that which "invented the priest." Figure that, as it evaporates it ignites the memories and regrets of believers, ex-believers and non-believers [*D'altronde la decisione più significativa del pontificato (di Francesco), quella contenuta in Evangelii Gaudium, non è stata ancora recepita dai vescovi: è quella che afferma che le conferenze episcopali hanno "autentica autorità dottrinale." Toccherebbe dunque ai vescovi episcopati sollevare un tema sul quale si gioca la vita delle loro chiese: ma l'indolenza prevale, incoraggiata dalla speranza che la riforma domani abbia lo stesso coraggio di quella che "inventò il prete". Figura che mentre svapora accende i ricordi e i rimpianti di credenti, ex credenti e non credenti*] (*Ibid*).

There is just one small matter in the way of "authentic doctrinal authority" for episcopal conferences such as the Zambia Conference of Catholic Bishops which would lead to the re-invention of the priesthood for the Zambian Church. According to canon 331, the Roman pontiff, "By virtue of his office he possesses supreme, full, immediate, and universal ordinary power in the Church, which he is always able to exercise freely" as he did in the standoff between the Vatican and the *Igboland* diocese of *Ahiara* in which Pope Francis blinked after reading them the riot act. For those not familiar with Nigerian geo-politics, in 1969 *Ahiara* was the epicentre of the *Biafran* uprising where the *Ahiara Declaration: The Principles of the Biafran Revolution*, a speech by the Head of State of *Biafra*, was made by Lieutenant Colonel Chukwuemeka Odumegwu Ojukwu. Francis had to walk back his threat to suspend any priest who did not personally write to him to promise obedience to him and to any bishop he would appoint. The diocese was boycotting the imposition of a priest from outside the diocese as bishop. The Pope has since reassigned the rejected bishop to a newly created diocese and *Ahiara* remains *sede vacante*.

In *Evangelii Gaudium*, Pope Francis gives the impression that this power has been devolved. This is clearly not the case since as the Pope says, "Yet this desire has not been fully realized, since a juridical status of episcopal conferences which would see them as subjects of specific attributions, including genuine doctrinal authority, has not yet been sufficiently elaborated. Excessive centralization, rather than proving helpful, complicates the Church's life and her missionary outreach" (*EG* 2013: par 32). For crying out loud, whose job is it and who should ensure full realisation of devolution? The Pope does not mention a canon I was not aware of even as a priest. "Clerics are bound by a special obligation to show reverence and obedience to the Supreme Pontiff and their own ordinary." If the Pope is committed to full devolution of his power and authority, canon 273 will need to go.

16. Two Strange Bedfellows in the Path of Bergoglian Reform

There are at least two strange bedfellows who are hell bent on thwarting Bergoglian reform, such as the one mentioned in *Evangelii Gaudium*, although they are on two extremes of the sexual continuum between straight and gay. I have described the two foes as the Vatican deep state and Vatican Lavender *Mafia* in my forthcoming book *Two Ships Same Storm and a Captain from the Ends of the Earth: Scandal and Priesthood in the Barque of St Peter*. In my research for the book, I discovered two ecclesiastical centres of power — real or virtual, which I have termed the Vatican deep state and Vatican Lavender *Mafia*. These are driven by at least seven vices: greed, pomp, clericalism, patriarchy, conservative and entrenched opposition to reform, homosexualisation of the Catholic priesthood as the new normal and the reversal of Vatican II.

From an African perspective, the gay variety is yet to break out in pandemic proportions as in Europe and the United States of America. But even in Africa, homosexualisation of the Catholic priesthood as the new normal is on the way, slowly but surely but I repeat I am not making moral judgement about sexual orientation. When that happens and it may be sooner rather than later, the challenge needs to be rephrased and clear guidelines given. I fear that the Benedict XVI era guidelines from the *Congregation for Catholic Education* (2005) on "norms concerning a specific question, made more urgent by the current situation, and that is: whether to admit to the seminary and to holy orders candidates who have deep-seated homosexual tendencies"[44] may not be adequate. The guidelines need to be brought up to speed in line with the Austrian experiment on the blessing of same sex couples but this is a can of worms I can ill afford to open.

17. Conclusion

This article took its point of departure from Pope Francis' concern about initial formation for the priesthood and suggests that in the light of the *Ratio Fundamentalis*, formation must operate on the principle of "small is beautiful" by avoiding mass manufacture of priests. The focus of such formation needs to be accompaniment and discernment. Failure to do this, we risk in the words of Pope Francis, churning out little monsters in circumstances that are akin to policing rather transformative formation. Pope Francis never defined what he meant by "little monsters" but I opine that it has to do with the style of leadership. Little or big monsters would be the equivalent of an ecclesiastical Donald Trump. These monsters eventually grow into big monsters as bishops, archbishops and cardinals with a heart of stone instead of a heart of flesh whose default exercise of authority is hard power rather than soft power. As the Pope says, formation and we might add episcopal oversight "is a work of art, not policing" [*è un'opera artigianale, non poliziesca*].[45]

This article has been something of a mixed bag or a Pandora's Box. Although broken, the system of formation still manages to produce masterpieces but one feels that like a student's evaluations I took part in, "the system can do better." Formation is a bit like preaching to the choir— at times challenging, especially when learning a difficult piece but generally lots of fun. The thought that a seminarian would be seated in front of a formator, not listening to Plato's allegory of the cave but worried that his holiday indiscretions with the village prostitute might be revealed any time. Our system ought to be open to such unfortunates if the potential is there, not automatic expulsion. At the same time, our system ought to be user-friendly enough for a young man too high on libido to own up and say, "Sorry, this is not for me but please can I complete my academic degree so that I can continue to serve the Church? While I am at it, may I get some help in psycho-sexual maturity so that I can at least learn to keep it in my trousers until the right moment and with the right person?" The system can then discuss who picks up the tab. Far too many sexually dysfunctional candidates and sexual perverts make it as celibates, while wearing two chastity belts and immediately after ordination, all hell breaking loose in the procreation department. As one bishop said of his procreating celibates in desperation, *mwachilamo fye. Mwachila ukufyala nabeene abaupana* [you have outdone even the married when it comes to procreating]. It was said of one seminarian in the 2000s, later ordained as a priest, that he had no problems with thirsting and yearning for alcohol, like most of his classmates. His only thirst and yearning had to do with satiating the nether regions and already was a closet dad with a "child of the ordained" who was not acknowledged for fear of expulsion. He has since been suspended from functioning as a priest, on account of his thirst and yearning, except as he knows, administering sacraments in *periculo mortis*. I am not sure whether he has owned up to his paternity.

References

Altman, James (30 August 2020), "Fr. Altman: You cannot be Catholic & a Democrat. Period. (Part I)," https://www.youtube.com/watch?v=3-7eoTN2vNM&feature=emb_logo (Accessed on 23.11.2020)

Ave Maria Press (2012), "What is the New Evangelization?" https://www.avemariapress.com/yearoffaith/what-is-the-new-evangelization/ (Accessed on 16.07.2020)

Baggini, Julian (12 May 2005), "Wisdom's folly: The unexamined life is not worth living — Plato," https://www.theguardian.com/theguardian/2005/may/12/features11.g24 (Accessed on 27.06.2020)

Communion and Liberation (2015), *Communion and Liberation: A Lay Movement*, Milan: Communion and Liberation

Congregation for Catholic Education (2005), "Instruction concerning the criteria for the discernment of vocations with regard to persons with homosexual tendencies in view of their admission to the seminary and to Holy Orders," http://www.vatican.va/roman_curia/congregations/ccatheduc/documents/rc_con_ccatheduc_doc_20051104_istruzione_en.html (Accessed on 24.04.2020)

Cooper-White, Pamela (7 July 2004), "Becoming a Clergy Mother: A Study of How Motherhood Changes Ministry," https://alban.org/archive/becoming-a-clergy-mother-a-study-of-how-motherhood-changes-ministry/ (Accessed on 29.06.2020)

di Francesco, Antonio Grana (3 January 20140, "Il Papa contro i pedofili nella Chiesa: 'Nei seminari sì ai peccatori, non ai corrotti,'" *Il Fatto Quotidiano*, https://www.ilfattoquotidiano.it/2014/01/03/il-papa-contro-i-pedofili-nella-chiesa-nei-seminarti-si-accettino-i-peccatori-non-i-corrotti/831108/ (Accessed on 25.11.2020)

Dillon-Malone, Clive (1987), "The Mutumwa Church of Peter Mulenga (Part II)," *Journal of Religion in Africa* 17 (1): 2–31

Eller, Cynthia (1991), "Relativizing the Patriarchy: The Sacred History of the Feminist Spirituality Movement," *History of Religions* 30(3): 279–295

Flynn, JD (14 July 2020), "Criticism of Cardinal Dolan letter 'silly,' Weigel publisher says," https://www.catholicnewsagency.com/news/criticism-of-cardinal-dolan-letter-silly-george-weigel-publisher-says-54781 (Accessed on 17.07.2020

Glatz, Carol (5 November 2014), "Pope: Bishops must be servants, not vain careerists after power, honor," *National Catholic Reporter*, https://www.ncronline.org/blogs/francis-chronicles/pope-bishops-must-be-servants-not-vain-careerists-after-power-honor (Accessed on 12.07.2020

Gula, Richard (2010), *Just Ministry: Professional Ethics for Pastoral Ministers*, New York: Paulist Press

Il Buongiorgio (13 March 2013), "*Habemus Papam Francesco*," http://www.buongiorgio.com/2013/03/habemus-papam-francesco.html (accessed on 21.05.2020)

Keyl, Steven (2017), "The Human Whisperer," https://www.stevenkeyl.com/the-human-whisperer/what-is-a-human-whisperer/ (Accessed on 01.07.2020)

McCarrick Report (2020), *Report on the Holy See's Institutional Knowledge and Decision-Making Related to Former Cardinal Theodore Edgar McCarrick* (*1930 to 2017*), http://www.vatican.va/resources/resources_rapporto-card-mccarrick_20201110_en.pdf (Accessed on 15.11.2020)

McElwee, Joshua J (14 July 2020), "Exclusive: Dolan sends book on 'The Next Pope' to cardinals around the world," *The National Catholic Reporter*, https://www.ncronline.org/news/people/exclusive-dolan-sends-book-next-pope-cardinals-around-world (Accessed on 16.07.2020)

McGarvey, Bill (4 January 2014), "Pope: Warns that Poorly Trained Priests Can Become 'Little Monsters'," *America the Jesuit Review*, https://www.americamagazine.org/content/all-things/pope-warns-poorly-trained-priests-can-become-little-monsters,%20accessed%20on%2030.05.2020 (Accessed on 05.06.2020

Melloni, Alberto (22 March 2017), "*La messa è finita. Così dopo cinque secoli tramonta la figura del prete* [The Mass is over. So, after five centuries the figure of the priest sets], *La Reppublica* posted by *Il Sismografico*, http://ilsismografo.blogspot.com/2017/03/italia-la-messa-e-finita.html (Accessed on 01.06.2020

Messainlatino (26 June 2020), "*Commissariati i Memores Domini di Comunione e Liberazione*?" http://blog.messainlatino.it/2020/06/breaking-news-commissariati-i-memores.html (Accessed on 08.07.2020)

Michello, Janet (2020), "The Black Madonna: A Theoretical Framework for the African Origins of Other World Religious Beliefs," *Religions* 11(10), file:///C:/Users/user/Downloads/religions-11-00511%20(1).pdf (Accessed on 25.11.2020)

Mukuka, Tarcisius (2020a), "Anatomy of an Episcopal Dressing down and Clericalism: A Prince of the Catholic Church and an Ecclesial Irritant," Munich: GRIN Verlag

Mukuka, Tarcisius (2020b), "Sexual Abuse in the Catholic Church Across the Big Pond: The Vicar of Christ, His Nemesis and a Prince's Scarlet Cardinal Sins," Munich: GRIN Verlag

Pentin, Edward (2 July 2020), "Vatican Appoints Canonist to Look into Communion and Liberation's Lay Association," *National Catholic Register*, https://www.ncregister.com/blog/edward-pentin/vatican-appoints-canonist-to-look-into-communion-and-liberations-lay-associ (Accessed on 08.07.2020)

Plato, *Apologia*, 37e–38b, http://www.perseus.tufts.edu/hopper/text?doc=plat.+apol.+38a (Accessed on 27.06.2020)

Pope, Alexander (1734), "An Essay on Man: Epistle II," https://www.poetryfoundation.org/poems/44900/an-essay-on-man-epistle-ii (Accessed on 27.06.2020)

Shaw, Russell (3 June 2002), "Clericalism and the Sex Abuse Scandal," America the Jesuit Review, https://www.americamagazine.org/issue/375/article/clericalism-and-sex-abuse-scandal (Accessed on 13.07.2020

Slater, Jennifer (2019), "The Catholic Church in need of de-clericalisation and moral doctrinal agency: Towards an ethically accountable hierarchical leadership," *HTS Teologiese Studies/Theological Studies* 75(4), https://hts.org.za/index.php/hts/article/view/5446/14118 (Accessed on 12.07.2020)

Spadaro, Antonio (4 January 2014), "'*Svegliate Il Mondo!*' *Colloquio di Papa Francesco con i Superiori Generali*," *La Civiltà Cattolica* 1:3–17, https://www.laciviltacattolica.it/articolo/svegliate-il-mondo-colloquio-di-papa-francesco-con-i-superiori-generali/ (Accessed on 05.06.2020)

Strynkowski, John J (15 July 2020), "George Weigel imagines the next Pope," *America the Jesuit Review*, https://www.americamagazine.org/faith/2020/07/15/george-weigel-imagines-next-pope (Accessed on 16.07.2020)

Tóth, Zita V (2020), "What is wrong with CL? Or, how not to Run a Catholic Community," http://zitavtoth.com/public/archive/cl/ (Accessed on 08.07.2020)

Verse by Verse Ministry International (2020), "Should we take literally Jesus' command to 'not call anyone on earth your father'?" https://www.versebyverseministry.org/bible-answers/should-we-take-literally-jesus-command-to-not-call-anyone-on-earth-your-fat (Accessed on 13.07.2020)

Weber, Maryasia (2009), "Significant Markers of Human Maturation Applied to the Selection and Formation of Seminarians," *Seminary Journal* 15(1): 35–41

Weigel, George (15 July 2020), "The Next Pope and Vatican II," *First Things*, https://www.firstthings.com/web-exclusives/2020/07/the-next-pope-and-vatican-ii (Accessed on 16.07.2020)

Winters, Michael Sean (6 July 2020), "Weigel's 'The Next Pope' has a crimped, Americanist vision of papacy," *National Catholic Reporter*, https://www.ncronline.org/news/opinion/distinctly-catholic/weigels-next-pope-has-crimped-americanist-vision-papacy (Accessed on 16.07.2020)

About the Author

Tarcisius Mukuka is a biblical exegete by training. His ideal job is research in the Humanities and Social Sciences. He holds a doctorate in Biblical Hermeneutics from the University of Surrey in the United Kingdom. His doctoral dissertation was entitled *Orality as Casualty: Contextual and Postcolonial Analysis of Biblical Hermeneutics in Bembaland* (2014). He is currently a senior lecturer in Religious Studies at Kwame Nkrumah University in Kabwe. He is also President of *Theologians against Violence*, a praxis-oriented think-tank with the immediate aim of contributing to free, fair, transparent and peaceful elections in Zambia; beginning with the 2021 General Elections. His research interests include apocalyptic literature, postcolonialism and the Bible, gender and the Bible, the Bible and Misogyny, religion, politics and power. He is the author of *Spoken Voice/Written Word: Negotiating How We Hear/Read the Bible* (2016) published by Lambert Academic Publishing and *In the Eye of a Very Catholic Storm* (forthcoming), by Crown Arts Publishers.

Endnotes

[1] Antonio Spadaro, 4 January 2014, "'*Svegliate Il Mondo*!' *Colloquio di Papa Francesco con i Superiori Generali*," *La Civiltà Cattolica* 1:3–17, https://www.laciviltacattolica.it/articolo/svegliate-il-mondo-colloquio-di-papa-francesco-con-i-superiori-generali/ (Accessed on 05.06.2020)

[2] As Clive Dillone-Malone explains, "The general term '*shing'anga*' covers a wide range of types of healers which includes the *katundula*, the *kabuka* and the *mucapi*. Hence, *shing'anga* in itself and without any further qualification refers to the category of 'healer' rather than to any particular form of healer. It includes the ability to divine the cause of the ill ness in question as well as to prescribe the appropriate kind of remedial treatment, whether herbal or otherwise (Dillon-Malone 1987: 14)."

[3] Tarcisius Mukuka (2020), *The Catholic Church, Use of Hard Power and the Appointment of Bishops: The Case of a Fictitious but Alas all too Familiar Scenario in Zambezia*, Munich: GRIN Verlag

[4] *Ibid*

[5] Tarcisius Mukuka (2020), "Anatomy of an Episcopal Dressing down and Clericalism: A Prince of the Catholic Church and an Ecclesial Irritant," Munich: GRIN Verlag, https://www.grin.com/document/948402

[6] Carol Glatz, 5 November 2014, "Pope: Bishops must be servants, not vain careerists after power, honour," *National Catholic Reporter*, https://www.ncronline.org/blogs/francis-chronicles/pope-bishops-must-be-servants-not-vain-careerists-after-power-honor (Accessed on 12.07.2020)

[7] Jennifer Slater (2019), "The Catholic Church in need of de-clericalisation and moral doctrinal agency: Towards an ethically accountable hierarchical leadership," *HTS Teologiese Studies/Theological Studies* 75(4), https://hts.org.za/index.php/hts/article/view/5446/14118 (Accessed on 12.07.2020)

[8] Papa Francesco (5 November 2014), "*Udienza Generale, Piazza San Pietro, Mercoledì, 5 novembre 2014*," http://www.vatican.va/content/francesco/it/audiences/2014/documents/papafrancesco_20141105_udienza-generale.html (Accessed on 22.11.2020)

[9] John J. Strynkowski, 15 July 2020, "George Weigel imagines the next Pope," *America the Jesuit Review*, https://www.americamagazine.org/faith/2020/07/15/george-weigel-imagines-next-pope (Accessed on 16.07.2020)

[10] *Ave Maria Press* (2012), "What is the New Evangelization?" https://www.avemariapress.com/yearoffaith/what-is-the-new-evangelization/ (Accessed on 16.07.2020)

[11] Michael Sean Winters, 6 July 2020, "Weigel's 'The Next Pope' has a crimped, Americanist vision of papacy," *National Catholic Reporter*, https://www.ncronline.org/news/opinion/distinctly-catholic/weigels-next-pope-has-crimped-americanist-vision-papacy (Accessed on 16.07.2020)

[12] *Ibid*

[13] Joshua J. McElwee, 14 July 2020, "Exclusive: Dolan sends book on 'The Next Pope' to cardinals around the world," *The National Catholic Reporter*, https://www.ncronline.org/news/people/exclusive-dolan-sends-book-next-pope-cardinals-around-world (Accessed on 16.07.2020)

[14] George Weigel, 15 July 2020, "The Next Pope and Vatican II," *First Things*, https://www.firstthings.com/web-exclusives/2020/07/the-next-pope-and-vatican-ii (Accessed on 16.07.2020)

[15] JD Flynn, 14 July 2020, "Criticism of Cardinal Dolan letter 'silly,' Weigel publisher says," https://www.catholicnewsagency.com/news/criticism-of-cardinal-dolan-letter-silly-george-weigel-publisher-says-54781 (Accessed on 17.07.2020)

[16] *Ibid*

[17] *Ibid*

[18] Swithan Kalobwe, 14 July 2024 email to me reflecting on the 1985 seminary boycott as someone who was in the eye of a very Catholic storm, to use the title of my forthcoming book.

[19] Image credit: http://google.com/search?tbm=isch&q=The+Horse+Whisperer (Accessed on 22.11.2020)

[20] Steven Keyl (2017), "The Human Whisperer," https://www.stevenkeyl.com/the-human-whisperer/what-is-a-human-whisperer/ (Accessed on 01.07.2020)

[21] *Verse by Verse Ministry International* (2020), "Should we take literally Jesus' command to 'not call anyone on earth your father'?" https://www.versebyverseministry.org/bible-answers/should-we-take-literally-jesus-command-to-not-call-anyone-on-earth-your-fat (Accessed on 13.07.2020)

[22] *Ibid*

[23] *Il Buongiorgio*, 13 March 2013, "*Habemus Papam Francesco*," http://www.buongiorgio.com/2013/03/habemus-papam-francesco.html (accessed on 21.05.2020)

[24] Antonio Spadaro, 4 January 2014, "'*Svegliate Il Mondo!' Colloquio di Papa Francesco con i Superiori Generali*," *La Civiltà Cattolica* 1:3–17, https://www.laciviltacattolica.it/articolo/svegliate-il-mondo-colloquio-di-papa-francesco-con-i-superiori-generali/ (Accessed on 05.06.2020)

[25] Bill McGarvey (4 January 2014), "Pope: Warns that Poorly Trained Priests Can Become 'Little Monsters'," *America the Jesuit Review*, https://www.americamagazine.org/content/all-things/pope-warns-poorly-trained-priests-can-become-little-monsters,%20accessed%20on%2030.05.2020 (Accessed on 05.06.2020)

[26] James Altman (30 August 2020), "Fr. Altman: You cannot be Catholic & a Democrat. Period. (Part I)," https://www.youtube.com/watch?v=3-7eoTN2vNM&feature=emb_logo (Accessed on 23.11.2020)

[27] *Ibid*

[28] William Callahan (9 September 2020), "La Crosse bishop to correct 'Catholics can't be Democrats' priest," *Catholic News Agency*, https://www.catholicnewsagency.com/news/la-crosse-bishop-to-correct-catholics-cant-be-democrats-priest-fr-james-altman-37520 (Accessed on 24.11.2020)

[29] Bill McGarvey (4 January 2014), "Pope: Warns that Poorly Trained Priests Can Become 'Little Monsters'," *America the Jesuit Review*, https://www.americamagazine.org/content/all-things/pope-warns-poorly-trained-priests-can-become-little-monsters,%20accessed%20on%2030.05.2020 (Accessed on 05.06.2020)

[30] Alberto Melloni, 22 March 2017, "*La messa è finita. Così dopo cinque secoli tramonta la figura del prete* [The Mass is over. So, after five centuries the figure of the priest sets], *La Reppublica* posted by *Il Sismografico*, http://ilsismografo.blogspot.com/2017/03/italia-la-messa-e-finita.html (Accessed on 01.06.2020)

[31] Allen, John L (12 November 2020), "History-making report sets a precedent the Vatican can't walk back," *Crux*, https://cruxnow.com/news-analysis/2020/11/history-making-report-sets-a-precedent-the-vatican-cant-walk-back/ (Accessed on 18.11.2020)
[32] Russell Shaw, 3 June 2002, "Clericalism and the Sex Abuse Scandal," America the Jesuit Review, https://www.americamagazine.org/issue/375/article/clericalism-and-sex-abuse-scandal (Accessed on 13.07.2020)
[33] *Ibid*
[34] *Ibid*
[35] Edward Pentin, 2 July 2020, "Vatican Appoints Canonist to Look into Communion and Liberation's Lay Association," *National Catholic Register*, https://www.ncregister.com/blog/edward-pentin/vatican-appoints-canonist-to-look-into-communion-and-liberations-lay-associ (Accessed on 08.07.2020)
[36] *Messainlatino*, 26 June 2020, "*Commissariati i Memores Domini di Comunione e Liberazione*?" http://blog.messainlatino.it/2020/06/breaking-news-commissariati-i-memores.html (Accessed on 08.07.2020)
[37] *Communion and Liberation* (2015), *Communion and Liberation: A Lay Movement*, Milan: Communion and Liberation, page 3
[38] Zita V. Tóth (2020), "What is wrong with CL? Or, how not to Run a Catholic Community," http://zitavtoth.com/public/archive/cl/ (Accessed on 08.07.2020)
[39] These markers were first described and presented in the chapter "Significant Markers of Human Maturation Applied to the Selection and Formation of Seminarians," Maryasia Weber (2009), *Seminary Journal* 15(1): 35–41
[40] Pamela Cooper-White (7 July 2004), "Becoming a Clergy Mother: A Study of How Motherhood Changes Ministry," https://alban.org/archive/becoming-a-clergy-mother-a-study-of-how-motherhood-changes-ministry/ (Accessed on 29.06.2020)
[41] Alexander Pope (1734), "An Essay on Man: Epistle II," https://www.poetryfoundation.org/poems/44900/an-essay-on-man-epistle-ii (Accessed on 27.06.2020)
[42] Julian Baggini (12 May 2005), "Wisdom's folly: The unexamined life is not worth living — Plato," https://www.theguardian.com/theguardian/2005/may/12/features11.g24 (Accessed on 27.06.2020)
[43] Plato, *Apologia*, 37e–38b, http://www.perseus.tufts.edu/hopper/text?doc=plat.+apol.+38a (Accessed on 27.06.2020)
[44] *Congregation for Catholic Education* (2005), "Instruction concerning the criteria for the discernment of vocations with regard to persons with homosexual tendencies in view of their admission to the seminary and to Holy Orders," http://www.vatican.va/roman_curia/congregations/ccatheduc/documents/rc_con_ccatheduc_doc_20051104_istruzione_en.html (Accessed on 24.04.2020)
[45] Antonio Grana di Francesco (3 January 20140, "Il Papa contro i pedofili nella Chiesa: 'Nei seminari sì ai peccatori, non ai corrotti,'" *Il Fatto Quotidiano*, https://www.ilfattoquotidiano.it/2014/01/03/il-papa-contro-i-pedofili-nella-chiesa-nei-seminarti-si-accettino-i-peccatori-non-i-corrotti/831108/ (Accessed on 25.11.2020)

YOUR KNOWLEDGE HAS VALUE

- We will publish your bachelor's and master's thesis, essays and papers

- Your own eBook and book - sold worldwide in all relevant shops

- Earn money with each sale

Upload your text at www.GRIN.com and publish for free